The All-Around Pumpkin Book

The All-Around Pumpkin Book

by Margery Cuyler

illustrated by
Corbett Jones

Holt, Rinehart and Winston | *New York*

Text copyright © 1980 by Margery Cuyler
Illustrations copyright © 1980 by Corbett Jones
All rights reserved, including the right to reproduce
this book or portions thereof in any form.
Published simultaneously in Canada by Holt, Rinehart
and Winston of Canada, Limited.
Printed in the United States of America

Library of Congress Cataloging in Publication Data

Cuyler, Margery.   The all-around pumpkin book.
Summary: Presents little-known facts about and
recipes and craft projects using pumpkins. Also
includes planting and cultivation hints and suggested
carving techniques.
1. Cookery (Pumpkin)—Juvenile literature.
2. Pumpkin—Juvenile literature. 3. Halloween
decorations—Juvenile literature. [1. Pumpkin.
2. Cookery—Pumpkin. 3. Halloween decorations.
4. Handicraft] I. Jones, Corbett. II. Title.
TX803.P93C89 1980b   641.3'5'62

  hc. ISBN 0-03-047101-X   79-4820   10 9 8 7 6 5 4 3 2 1
  pbk. ISBN 0-03-056818-8   79-3532   10 9 8 7 6 5 4 3 2 1

For Jan, my pumpkin man,
and for the pumpkin lady

Acknowledgments

The author would like to thank Eugenia Worman for contributing the planting and cultivation section and some of the original recipes in this book. She would also like to thank the Worman family for eating pumpkin dishes daily; Jamie and Juliana McIntyre, Sarah Perkins, and Jenny Hawkes for carving pumpkins; Mary Combs for her helpful suggestions; Mary Mason of Miss Mason's School in Princeton, New Jersey, for her cooperation and encouragement; and Roth Wilkofsky, Richard Hutton, and the Worman children for contributing pumpkin jokes.

Contents

Introduction

꿎꿎꿎 "Pumpkin" comes from a Greek work, *pepon,* meaning a large melon. Pumpkins were a favorite garden vegetable of the American settlers. Rich in phosphorus, calcium, iron, and vitamins A and C, they were a healthy addition to the diet. The early Americans ate so much pumpkin that they used to sing, "We have pumpkin at morning and pumpkin at noon; If it was not for pumpkin, we would be undoon." The settlers learned how to grow and use pumpkins from the Indians.

The Indians planted them in mounds among their corn. It was difficult to clear land, and they could save space by mixing their crops together. The Indians added pumpkin pieces to their stews and fed raw pumpkin chunks to their horses.

There are two groups of pumpkins: the orange stock pumpkin and the yellow cheese pumpkin. Cheese pumpkins are canned and sold as pie fillings. Stock pumpkins are the kind the Indians grew. Today, they are used as food for livestock or for making jack-o'-lanterns. Big Max, Connecticut Field, and Jack-o'-lantern are the best-known types of stock pumpkins. Their roundish shapes, bright colors, and soft insides make them ideal for carving.

It's unclear whether the pumpkin came to North and South America from Asia or the other way around. Pumpkin seeds have been found in ancient Asian ruins. Also, the first American Indians came from northeast Asia. They came to North America across the Bering Strait in 13,000 B.C. Perhaps they brought the pumpkin with them. Pumpkin seeds have been found in prehistoric Indian cliff dwellings in Colorado. They have also been found in Peruvian ruins that date back to 1800 B.C. The pumpkin was probably grown centuries ago in Africa and Indochina as well, since it is mentioned in the myths of the people there. For example, the races now living in eastern Indochina are said to have come out of a pumpkin. And in Africa, there is a Swahili story about a patch of pumpkins that sprang up where the Devil or *Zimwi* died. Although the pumpkin's origin is unknown, experts agree that Indians were growing pumpkins for hundreds of years before the first Europeans came to America.

A pumpkin can be used for many things. It can be carved into a jack-o'-lantern, stewed for cooking (New Englanders coined the phrase "softer than stewed pumpkin"), and used for curing illness. Pumpkin seed tea, for example, is supposed to be good for the bladder and for killing tapeworm. In the eighteenth century, the pumpkin was used for cutting hair! The males in New England turned pumpkin shells upside down on their heads before having a haircut. The hair was trimmed from around the base of the shell. This is where the expression "pumpkinhead" comes from.

Things can even be hidden in pumpkins! On January 21, 1950, a man named Alger Hiss was sentenced to five years in prison. He was accused of having lied about passing secret

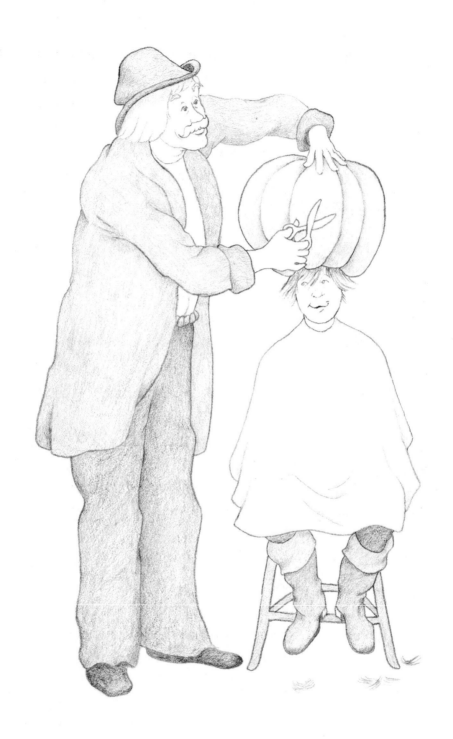

papers to the Communists while working for the State Department in 1938. The man who accused him was an ex-Communist named Whittaker Chambers. In court, Mr. Chambers produced microfilm of the papers that he said Mr. Hiss had given to the Russians. Mr. Chambers had kept the microfilm hidden in a pumpkin on his farm in Maryland.

Pumpkins have appeared in many famous stories. Cinderella rides to a ball in a pumpkin that has been changed into an elegant coach by her fairy godmother. In a popular tall tale told in the southern part of the United States, a numskull finds a pumpkin lying in the road. He thinks it's an egg that has been laid by a donkey and throws it into some bushes. When a frightened rabbit runs out, the numskull mistakes it for the donkey's colt! And Linus in the cartoon strip *Peanuts* waits patiently in a pumpkin patch on Halloween night for "the Great Pumpkin."

There are several big festivals that have been held in honor of the pumpkin. In the nineteenth century, there was a famous *Fête du Poitron* (Festival of the Pumpkin) in Paris. When the biggest pumpkin was chosen, it was given a tinsel-and-paper crown. Then it was marched around the market, where everyone bowed before it. Finally, it was cut into pieces, which were then sold for making soup.

Two of America's largest pumpkin festivals are in Illinois. This is not surprising, since most of America's pumpkins come from Illinois, Ohio, and Indiana. Eureka, Illinois boasts that it is the pumpkin capital of the world. Every fall, the town

has a great celebration at which as many as ten thousand pumpkin pies are given away. There's enough dough in them to cover half a city block! The high point of the festival is the crowning of the festival queen. She arrives at the courthouse in a coach drawn by four horses. A footman opens the coach door, and the queen, in a glittering gown, steps down to a plush carpet. Then she mounts a platform decorated with pumpkins to receive her crown. On the next night, she rides through the town on a beautiful float that's part of a parade.

Perhaps the best-known celebration is in Sycamore, Illinois. A local service club gives away five tons of pumpkins to the town. Then everyone tackles them with knives, paint, felt-tip markers, bags of vegetables, and household items. They are made into many different kinds of pumpkin sculptures and jack-o'-lanterns. A few days before Halloween, decorated

pumpkins are placed on the lawn of the De Kalb County Court-house. Some of the larger ones have to be brought in baby carriages, wheelbarrows, and grocery carts! Prizes are given to the best. Then everyone goes to the arts and crafts exhibits, joins the pie-baking contests, and finally watches a big parade.

Jack-o'-lanterns themselves have a colorful history. The first ones were made from potatoes or the rinds of turnips. This custom dates back to an Irish legend about a stingy ne'er-do-well named Jack.

On Halloween night, he invited the Devil to have a drink with him.

"I'll only join you if you pay," said the Devil.

"Why should I do that?" bellowed Jack. "You're the Devil!

16

You can change into any shape that you like. Well, then, change into a sixpence, and we can pay for the drinks with that."

"What a clever idea," said the Devil, and he turned himself into a sixpence. Jack quickly dropped the sixpence into his pocket since it had a cross on it, and devils are afraid of crosses.

"Let me out!" screamed the Devil.

"Not unless you promise to leave me alone for a year," said Jack, laughing.

The Devil shouted and yelled, but finally agreed to the promise.

A year later, the Devil came looking for Jack. He found him under an apple tree.

"A year's up, and I've come for your soul," said the Devil.

"Fair is fair," said Jack. "But before I give you my soul, I'd like to ask you one last favor."

"And what's that?" asked the Devil.

"That you fetch me an apple from the apple tree, so that I won't get hungry in Hell."

"So be it," said the Devil, and he climbed the tree. Jack immediately carved a cross on the trunk.

"You've tricked me again!" shouted the Devil.

"Ah, yes," said Jack, "but I'll let you get down if you spare me for another ten years!"

And the Devil had to agree.

But Jack's good luck soon ran out. Before a year had passed, he died. And when he got to the gates of Heaven, he was turned away because all his life he had been stingy and mean.

"If Heaven won't take me, then I'll have to live in Hell," said Jack.

But when he reached the gates of Hell, the Devil was waiting for him.

"Go away!" shouted the Devil. "Don't you remember my promise? I can't claim your soul for another nine years."

"Promises can be broken," said Jack.

"No," said the Devil. "You're not wanted in Heaven, and you're not wanted in Hell. Not even nine years from now will I let you in. You deserve to be punished for all your tricks!"

"But where am I to go?" wailed Jack.

"You'll have to roam the earth," said the Devil.

"But what will I use for light?" asked Jack. "It's dark and lonely roaming the earth."

"Here," said the Devil, and he threw him a hot piece of coal. Jack put it in a turnip, and ever since, he's been wandering the earth with his jack-o'-lantern, looking for a place to rest.

Like the Irish, the Scots used turnips to make their jack-o'-lanterns. When they lit the candle inside, they'd carry the turnip like a lantern, hoping to scare away evil spirits. They called these jack-o'-lanterns "bogies."

English children used to use mangel-wurzels, a kind of beet with a large root. They hollowed them out and made a window for the candlelight to shine through.

The belief that jack-o'-lanterns warded off evil spirits dates back to before Christ. The Celts, who lived in what is now France and the British Isles, celebrated a harvest festival on October 31. It was known as *Samhain* or Summer's End. Everyone gathered together to feast on the food grown over the summer. But it was not an altogether joyous occasion. With the end of summer came the darkness of winter. The sun went into hiding, and dead souls came back to their former homes. The evil souls returned as witches and ghosts, fairies and goblins. Druids, or high priests, built great fires on the hills and moors. These were to honor the sun god and to protect the people from the bad spirits. People hollowed out turnips and put a lit candle inside. They carried these "lanterns" if they went outside. They thought the light would keep away the evil spirits.

American children don't have to use turnips, potatoes, or beets for jack-o'-lanterns on Halloween. When their ancestors came to America, they discovered that pumpkins were better suited for that purpose.

Now that you've learned some facts about pumpkins, you may want to try growing them or using them for cooking or crafts projects. However, working with pumpkins isn't as easy as it looks. A project like making a pumpkin totem pole is

sometimes hard and takes time and patience. Or cooking pumpkin recipes, which is fun, can be dangerous if safety rules aren't followed. Even carving pumpkins is difficult, since it's hard to control the knife blade. So, before you begin, ask an adult if he or she can help out.

Planting Guide

⋦§⋦§⋦§Pumpkins are the hogs of the vegetable world. They love to eat and drink, and their growth depends upon a hearty diet. The earth where they grow must be damp and full of plant food. (Pumpkins are 90 percent water and draw a lot of moisture from the soil.) Pumpkins also need at least six hours of sunlight a day. If you have a sunny backyard, are willing to feed and water the plants, and don't mind watching for weeds and bugs, you can become an outstanding pumpkin grower.

Buying Seeds

Order pumpkin seeds from a catalog or buy them at a hardware store, supermarket, small grocery store, garden center, or even a ten-cent store. Two well-known seed companies are W. Atlee Burpee Co., 300 Park Avenue, Warminster, Pennsylvania 18974 and G. W. Park Seed Co., Greenwood, South Carolina 29647.

Types of Seeds

There are many different types of seeds. Big Max, Connecticut Field, and Jack-o'-lantern seeds grow into stock pumpkins. These make good pumpkins for carving. Big Max are the largest and have been known to grow to over two hundred pounds. There is nothing quite like growing one of these giants and

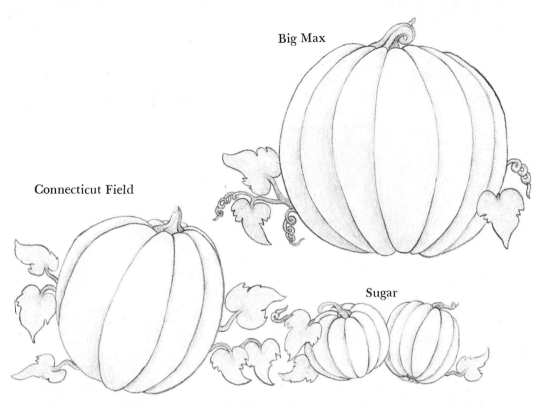

Big Max

Connecticut Field

Sugar

winning a contest. Since the pulp of the Big Max is stringy and tasteless, this pumpkin is not good for eating. Connecticut Field and Jack-o'-lantern grow large, too, but not as large as the Big Max. Unlike the Big Max, they can be eaten. Other pumpkin seeds are labeled Sugar Pumpkin, Small Sugar, or Funny Face, and these are the cheese pumpkins. They are grown mainly for eating, but can be carved as well. In general, the smaller the pumpkin, the better the flavor. People usually save these smaller pumpkins for cooking.

When to Plant
Read on the back of the seed package how many days the pumpkin needs for growing. Pumpkins don't like frost and must

be grown between the last frost of spring and the first frost of autumn. Call the weather bureau or ask a longtime gardener for the frost dates in your area.

Most stock pumpkins need 120–140 frost-free days, while cheese pumpkins need about 90. In a region with only 100 frost-free days, therefore, it's better to choose a cheese variety. Or else start stock pumpkin seeds indoors on a sunny window-sill before the last frost (see p. 27). Later, when frost season is past, they can be transplanted to the garden.

Where to Plant

Seeds should be planted *at the edge* of a garden. This is so that their vines, which sometimes grow as long as thirty feet, can be trained to grow into the grass alongside. Otherwise, they should be planted in a separate plot by themselves. The plot needs to be away from buildings and tall trees so that it gets lots of sun. If the plot is slanted, plant the seeds at the top of the slope, since frost settles first in low areas.

Making Hills

The next step is to "make hills" in which the seeds will be planted. First, dig up the soil in the area you've chosen for growing pumpkins. The best machine for doing this is a rotary cultivator, a large digging gadget with a motor. It has strong

24

steel spikes that turn and plunge into the soil, ripping the dirt apart and chopping it up. It has to be pushed over the garden plot several times to make the soil fine enough for planting. Rotary cultivators can be rented or bought from your local garden center. Check the local newspapers for ads.

When your patch is tilled, rake the soil, removing all debris and stones. Then measure circles about four feet (1.2 m) across for small cheese pumpkins, and six feet (1.8 m) across for large stock ones. (Circles for Big Max should be eight feet—2.4 m— across.) Within these circles, heap up the soil with your hands so that each circle looks like a low-lying hill or mound. This

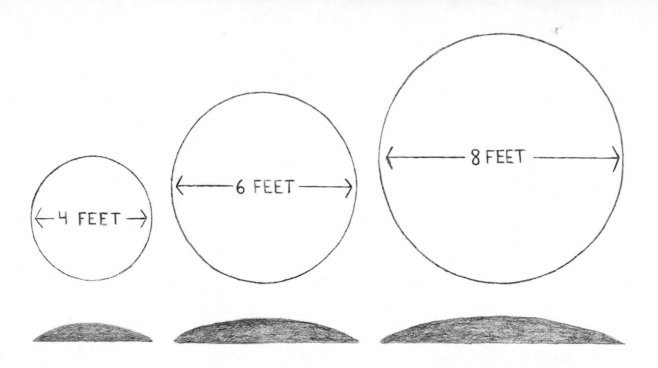

process of making hills is done so that seeds will have extra loose soil in which to begin their life.

Fertilizing

Now the hills should be fertilized. Supermarkets, garden centers, and hardware stores carry 50 or 100 pound (22.5 or 45 kg) bags of dried manure. Simply shovel this onto the marked hills —a bushel (35 1) a hill for stock varieties, half a bushel (17.5 1) for cheese ones.

If animal manure is used, it should sit around for six months first. Poultry manure should be left even longer—for at least a year.

When trying to grow the largest pumpkin in the neighborhood, it's a good idea to use three extra fertilizers: bone meal, lime, and compost. A sprinkling of bone meal, a handful of

26

lime, and a shovelful of compost should be enough. Bone meal is a white, powdery fertilizer that comes in a small bag. Lime is ground-up limestone and is also white and powdery and comes in a bag. Bone meal and lime can be bought at a hardware store. Compost is made from mixing garbage, manure, and other materials (such as dead leaves and grass) with dirt. The mixture should sit around for six months to a year until it rots. If you don't have any compost, ask a friendly gardener to give you some.

How to Prepare Seeds for Planting
If you want seeds to sprout quickly, soak them in lukewarm water the day before planting. You can also roll them up in wet paper towels. Soaked seeds should sprout in about five days. Unsoaked ones should appear in a week to ten days.

How to Plant Seeds Indoors Before the Last Frost
1. Six weeks before the last frost, fill several empty one-half-gallon (1.9 1) milk cartons with potting soil from the ten-cent store to a half inch (1.25 cm) from the top.
2. Poke holes in the bottoms of the cartons.

3. Put two seeds (soaked) in each carton and cover with an inch (2.5 cm) of soil. Press the soil lightly with your fingers.

4. Pour 1 cup (240 ml) of water down the inside edge of each carton so it doesn't disturb the seeds. Then sprinkle a little water over the top of the soil.

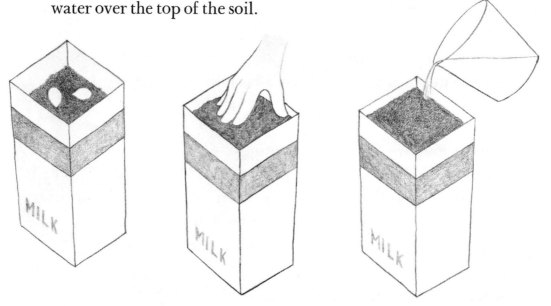

5. Cover the cartons with plastic wrap. Secure the wrap with elastic bands, if necessary.

6. Put the cartons on a tray in a warm place, 70° F (21° C). A good spot is near a radiator, hot-water heater, or furnace vent.

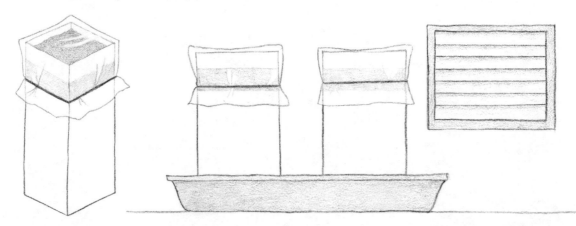

7. When the seeds sprout, remove the plastic wrap. Put the cartons on a sunny windowsill.

8. After a week of growing, snip off the smaller of the two plants in each carton.

9. For the next three or four weeks, water each plant every other day with one cup (240 ml) of water.

10. Two weeks before outdoor planting time, move the cartons outside to a sunny, protected spot. Cover them at night. This lets the plants get used to the outdoors and toughens them a little before they're on their own in a real garden.

11. After you have prepared your hills for outdoor planting, use a spade to dig one hole in the middle of each hill. The holes should be larger than the cartons. Next, soak the seedlings with lots of water and cut one side off each carton. Then slide the plants, dirt and all, into each hole. Press the soil around the seedlings so their roots are well covered. Water them again thoroughly.

Warning: Be sure to transplant the young seedlings on a rainy or cloudy day, or in the evening. Never transplant them in the direct sun, or they will wilt and stop growing for a while.

How to Plant Seeds That Have Not Been Started Indoors
You'll need eight seeds to a hill for the cheese variety, three to five seeds for the stock. Place them on the soil in a circle, leaving four inches (10 cm) between seeds. This is so the sprouts will have plenty of room for growing. After covering the seeds with an inch (2.5 cm) of dirt, press down lightly with the palm of your hand. Then sprinkle a little water on the hill.

Cheese

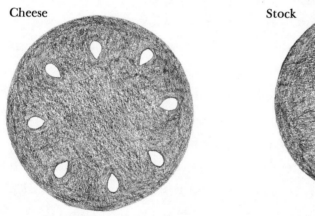

Stock

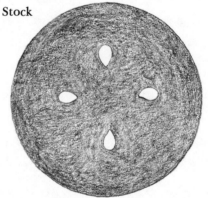

First Sprouts
When the seeds sprout, they push a pair of flat, thick leaves on a solid stem through the loose dirt. Then, for the next few days, they seem to be doing nothing. Actually, they are preparing to sprout their next leaves, which appear one by one. These

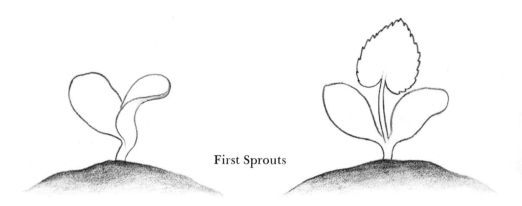

First Sprouts

are thinner, with a rough edge. From now on, the leaves will be exact copies of the rough-edged ones.

If it hasn't been raining during this early stage, the seedlings will need water. Without it, they won't grow, and if the soil is really dry, they will wilt.

Weeding

When the seedlings have their third and fourth leaves, weeds will start to pop up. Pull these right away before they get a chance to grow and crowd the pumpkin plants, or use a hoe to keep the soil around the plants chopped up. This will prevent new weeds from getting started.

Thinning

As the fourth and fifth leaves break out, some plants will seem healthier than others. Plants that are puny or have yellowed leaves must be removed and thrown away. This process is called thinning, and it is absolutely necessary. In the hills where cheese pumpkin seeds have been planted, leave the three best plants. But if you are growing Big Max or other very large stock pumpkins, *leave only one plant per hill.* This is so the vine will have the fertilizer all to itself.

Cheese   Stock

Watering

The more water pumpkins get, the better. They should have at least two inches of water a week. Water the plants with a hose, if possible, so that you can avoid stepping over the vines. The water from the hose should run into the hill for twenty minutes. Water once a week, unless it has been rainy. If you don't own a hose, fill a bucket with about half a gallon (1.9 l) of water and soak the hill. After August 1st, increase the amount to a gallon (3.8 l).

Pumpkin roots spread just under the soil's surface. They seldom grow more than eight inches (20 cm) deep. If you soak

the hills thoroughly, the roots should have a fine, soggy bed all season. Soak the hills before mulching.

Mulching

Mulching is when you cover the ground around plants to prevent weeds from growing. It also keeps the ground from drying out in the sun, since the sun's rays can't burn through it.

It is extremely important to mulch pumpkins. Once the vines grow long, it is hard to walk or move between them to pull the weeds. Also, you are likely to step on the vines by accident, damaging the stems or leaves.

The most common mulches are old newspapers, black plastic that comes in rolls and is sold at garden centers, thick piles of hay, grass clippings, wood chips, and leaves.

First, clean up the pumpkin household, removing the weeds. If you're using newspapers as your mulch, dampen them and

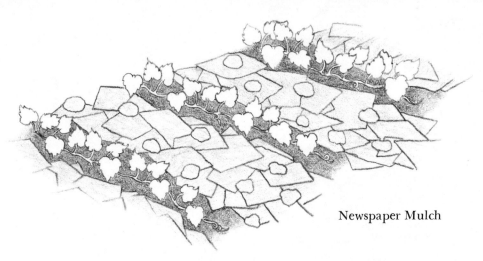

Newspaper Mulch

spread them thickly on the ground. The edges should overlap and be weighted down with rocks. If you're using hay, grass clippings, leaves, or chips, spread them thickly also. A few more weeds might begin to grow through the mulch; pull them out, and then add more mulch.

Plastic is rolled down the rows and held in place with rocks. A few slits cut here and there will allow rainwater to get through.

Leave some space around the base of the pumpkin vines so you can water them.

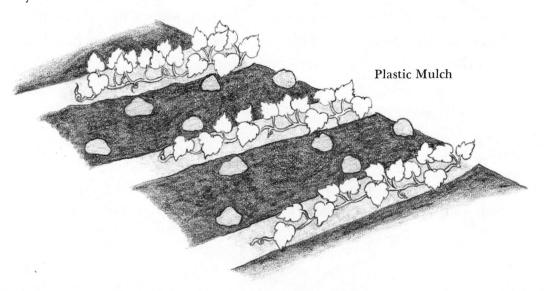

Plastic Mulch

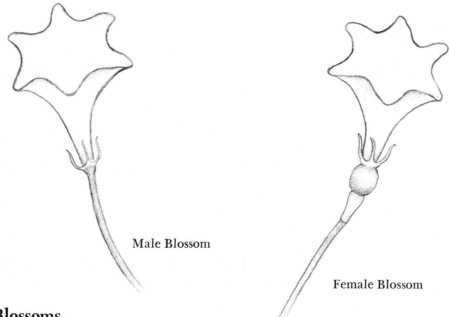

Male Blossom

Female Blossom

Blossoms

About a month after planting, big orange flowers will appear. These are male blossoms. They will shrivel up and die without fruiting. Male blossoms show up long before female ones. Female blossoms will appear about four weeks later. Pumpkins will develop at the base of the female blossoms only.

When the female blossoms turn up on the cheese pumpkin vines, let the pumpkins underneath grow. But on the stock vines, remove all the flowers except for one. There should be no more than one pumpkin per stock vine. Also, cut off excess branchings to prevent new vines with flowers from forming.

The main vines will continue growing beyond the point where the young pumpkins have begun their lives.

Bugs

When the pumpkin vines have been growing for about a month, they will probably be attacked by bugs. There is only one bug to watch out for—the squash vine borer. This is a moth whose eggs hatch on squash stems. Then the borers work their way into the stalk and feed. The pumpkin's leaves suddenly wilt, and there are tiny holes in the stalks that ooze a yellowish-green liquid. For this, you need Rotenone, a plant poison. It's the best kind to use, since it's less poisonous than other types. It is a white powder that comes in a can with holes in the top. It is sold wherever seeds are sold, including mail-order companies. Every five days or so, shake the Rotenone lightly over the stalks and leaves of your pumpkin plants. It may take only two or three dustings until the borers give up. There's no need to worry about other insects, such as white flies or Japanese beetles. They will not do enough harm to require dusting.

Weekly Feeding Program

From here on, the main work of pumpkin care is over. Cheese pumpkins don't need watering anymore unless there is a dry spell. However, stock pumpkins should be put on a weekly feeding program. This is especially true if you're growing a Big Max. A Big Max has a lot of growing to do in a short time.

Either make manure tea or use commercial fertilizer. Manure tea is a mixture of one part manure to ten parts of water. Commercial fertilizer, such as Rapid-Gro, is sold at plant and

Manure Tea

Commercial Fertilizer

supply stores. It's a green powder which you mix, according to the label's instructions, with a certain amount of water. One-half gallon (1.9 l) of either kind of fertilizer should be applied to the base of each hill every two weeks.

Turning the Big Max

A Big Max can grow up to be lopsided if it's not turned. The part resting on the ground becomes flat unless it gets sun. To prevent this, turn the pumpkin gently every week so that a different side faces the sun. Be careful not to let it break off from its stem.

Feeding Pumpkins with Sugar Water or Milk

To make pumpkins grow faster, try feeding them milk or one cup (240 mm) of water mixed with one tablespoon (15 ml) of sugar through a slit in their stalks. This method seems to work, causing some pumpkins to double their size in just a few days.

When a pumpkin is cantaloupe size, take a penknife and cut into a side of the vine, three inches (7.5 cm) from the fruit. Be careful not to cut through to the other side! Insert a six-inch

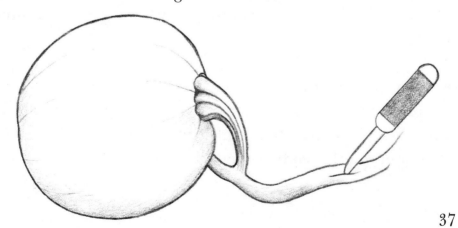

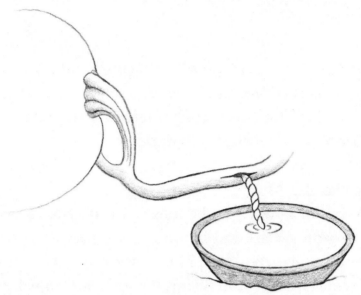

(15 cm) piece of lamp or candle wick, making sure that at least a quarter of an inch (6.25 mm) is firmly inside. Now, scoop out a hole in the dirt next to the pumpkin vine big enough for a cereal bowl. Fill the bowl with milk or sugar water. Place the bowl in the hole. Put the other end of the wick into the bowl. Try to cover the bowl with plastic so that dirt doesn't sift in. If you are using sugar water, stir it two or three times a day to keep the sugar from settling to the bottom.

Keep checking the arrangement. The milk may sour or the wick may fall out of the pumpkin. Replace the water or milk as it disappears. Feed your pumpkin sugar water or milk until you're ready to pick it.

Beating the Last Frost
To protect your pumpkin from an early frost, rearrange the vine. Pick it up and drape it in a circle around the pumpkin. Don't worry if the tendrils clinging to the mulch or grass break

off. It is not harmful to tear them. You may have to move the pumpkin closer to the center of its hill (if it isn't too large to lift by now). Cover both the vine and the pumpkin every night with a piece of plastic or a blanket. Secure the plastic by placing rocks along the edge, or the wind will blow it off. Remove the plastic during the daytime. Otherwise the plastic will heat up in the sun and burn the leaves underneath.

The pumpkin is ready to pick when you're ready to pick it!

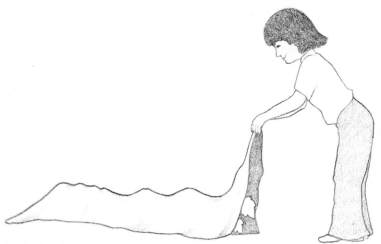

A Pumpkin's Life Span

Carved pumpkins usually don't last more than four days before they shrivel. But uncut pumpkins, protected from frost and kept in a cool place (40°F, 4.4° C), remain firm for about two months. Then their skin begins to bruise from the pressure of whatever they're resting upon. These soft spots mark the beginning of the end. When a pumpkin begins to soften and is the kind that can be cooked, cut out the spoiled part and save the rest for a recipe.

How to Carve a Pumpkin

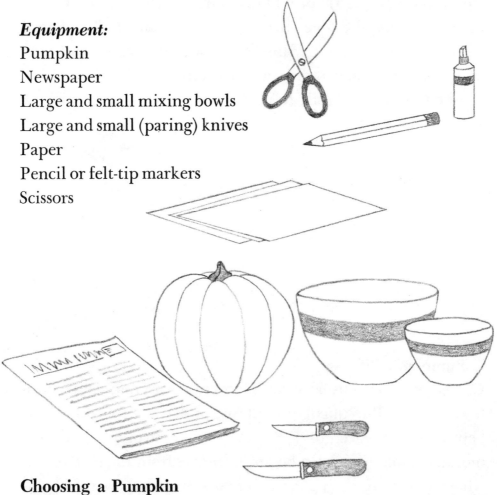

Equipment:
Pumpkin
Newspaper
Large and small mixing bowls
Large and small (paring) knives
Paper
Pencil or felt-tip markers
Scissors

Choosing a Pumpkin

Do you want a happy pumpkin? A sad pumpkin? A pumpkin with big jaws? A scary, mean pumpkin? A pumpkin with a stomachache? The shape of a pumpkin will give you ideas for the expression you want it to have. Round pumpkins suggest happy faces since they look happy even before they're carved! Tall, thin pumpkins are good for scary expressions, since there's room at the bottom for an extra long mouth with lots of jagged teeth. But any pumpkin, no matter what its shape or size, will take on the personality you give it.

First of all, choose a pumpkin that you like. There are many different sizes and shapes in the stores or farmers' markets before Halloween. No matter whether you buy or grow your pumpkin, it shouldn't be carved until right before you need it —four days ahead at the most. Jack-o'-lanterns spoil easily!

Choosing a Face

After you decide on the type of face you want, practice drawing it on a piece of paper. The bigger you make the features, the more the light will shine through when the jack-o'-lantern's lit. Now look at the drawing. Do you like it? Did you give your pumpkin enough scraggly teeth? Or a big enough smile? Eyebrows and ears? Be sure not to draw the mouth too close to the bottom, or it will be hard to see after the pumpkin's carved. If you're satisfied, then it's time to copy your drawing onto the pumpkin. Also, draw a circle around the stem. Make it big enough so that once it's cut, you can stick your hand through the hole and wiggle it around.

If you have trouble thinking up a face on your own, the designs below might be helpful. You can copy a face onto a piece of paper—but make sure the features are the right size for

your particular pumpkin. Cut them out and glue them into place. When the pumpkin is being carved, the knife should follow the edge of the paper.

Carving the Lid
Lay a lot of newspaper under the pumpkin, since carving is a messy business. Then hold the pumpkin firmly in place with both hands while a grown-up inserts the larger knife into the line you've drawn around the stem. The tip should be pointed

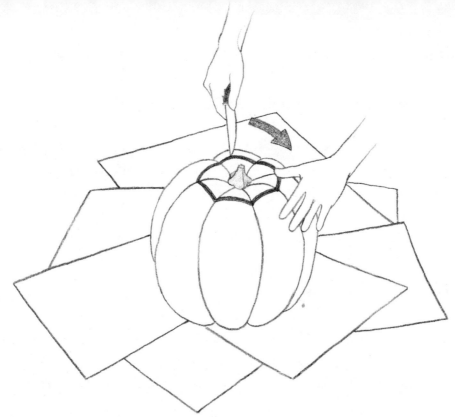

at a downward angle toward the center of the pumpkin. The pumpkin should be turned as it is cut until the lid can be pulled free.

Pulling Out the Pulp

The next step is really sloppy. Be prepared to get slimy, gooey hands and arms, and orange fingernails. Take the lid off the pumpkin and reach in. Pull out as much of the stringy pulp as you can and put it in the big bowl. Sometimes it's hard to break the pulp loose from the sides. Someone stronger may have to loosen it with the paring knife. Then take the big spoon and scoop out what's left. Scrape the bottom. Scrape the sides. The sides and bottom should look smooth, white, and dry. This takes a lot of work!

Saving the Seeds

There are hundreds of slippery pumpkin seeds mixed in with the pulp. These can be eaten later on or used for crafts projects. If you want to save them for cooking or making things, pick them out and put them in the small bowl.

Carving the Face

Carving the features isn't easy, especially if your pumpkin has skinny, pointed teeth, teeny-tiny eyes with eyeballs, or a button nose. The smaller the features, the harder they are to carve. Taking the paring knife, an adult should cut along the lines that you've drawn. When there's a large area to cut out, like a mouth, it's easier to divide it into sections and carve out one section at a time.

As soon as a chunk has been carved out, either push it in, so that it falls to the bottom of the inside, or pull it out with the tip of the knife blade. Perhaps if you're carving a small stock pumpkin, you'll want to save the chunks for cooking later on. Now you'll begin to see open spaces, and finally the pumpkin's face will emerge.

When the carving is finished, take a look at the pumpkin. Does it look like your drawing? Or did it change personality while it was being carved? There is no way you can fail at what you've done. A carved pumpkin is a work of art. The face you've made is different from anyone else's. And when its features are lit up by a candle inside, it will take on still another personality. There is nothing more wonderful than looking up at a window or walking toward a porch and seeing a jack-o'-lantern winking at you.

More Faces Than One?

You can carve a different face on each side of the pumpkin. When you get tired of looking at one face, just turn your pumpkin to the other one.

Dressing Up the Features

Add character to your jack-o'-lantern by dressing up its features with vegetables and household goods. Use your imagination! Anything you try will look interesting. A list of ideas follows.

Break toothpicks in half and use them to hold things in place. *Warning:* Don't light a candle inside the pumpkin if you attach paper goods to its outside.

Eyes
Mushrooms
Marshmallows
Cotton balls
Apples
Cranberries
Raisins

Noses
Cucumbers
Carrots
Toilet paper tubes
Celery

Mouths
Green beans
Carrots
Pipe cleaners
Celery

Teeth
Corn kernels
Marshmallows
Raisins
Cranberries

Ears
Apples
Mushrooms
Peppers
Marshmallows
Cotton balls
Cupcake papers
Paper cups

Eyebrows
Macaroni
Cranberries
Raisins
Marshmallows

Hats
Paper plates
Pie tins
Cupcake papers
Paper cups

Eyeglasses and pipes
Pipecleaners

Hair, Beards, Mustaches
Apple skins
Orange skins
Lettuce
Fireproof crepe
  paper cut into
  strips
Construction paper
  cut into strips

Painting a Pumpkin

Painting extra details on a jack-o'-lantern can be fun, too. Just draw them lightly onto the skin. Then fill them in with poster or powder paint or felt-tip markers.

Vegetable Peeler Features

You can also create features and designs by peeling away the orange skin where you've drawn your lines. This is a nice way of showing off the white flesh underneath. When the candle is lit, a soft light glows through the bald areas.

Votive Candle

Candles

Any kind of candle may be used inside a pumpkin, but votive candles last the longest (about 2½ hours). A votive candle is short and usually sits in a glass cup that catches the wax. Votive candles can be bought in most ten-cent stores.

Or use two candles. When the first candle's lit, tilt it over the opening on top, so that wax drips to the bottom. Then place the other candle in the melted wax. As the wax hardens, the candle will stay put. When it's lit, the wax will drip down the candle's edge and secure it to the base.

Another way to secure the candle is to carve a hole the size of the candlestick through the bottom of the pumpkin. Stick the candle through, so that its bottom rests on the ground.

Instead of Carving

Some people don't like to carve pumpkins. They prefer to decorate them with vegetables or paint. One advantage to this is that these pumpkins last longer than jack-o'-lanterns.

48

Cooking Equipment You Will Need

Shortening

Saucepans

Plastic wrap

Four dessert bowls

Two 9-inch (22.5 cm) single layer cake pans

Wire racks—2

Nut chopper

Blender

Colander

Large frying pan

Mixing bowls

Paring knife

Knife

Tall glasses

Electric mixer

Sieve

Wax paper

Metal mixing spoon

Cookie sheet

9-inch (22.5 cm) pie pans

Loaf pan—9″ x 5″ x 3″
(22.5 x 12.5 x 7.5 cm)

Fork

Spatulas

Rectangular baking pan—
9″ x 13″ x 2″
(22.5 x 32.5 x 5 cm)

Grater

Cutting board

Measuring spoons

Eggbeater

Measuring cups

1 qt. (.95 1) casserole dish

Cooking Up a Storm

❧❧❧Pumpkin filling by itself tastes bland. Without cinnamon, nutmeg, ginger, and other spices, pumpkin dishes would be very dull indeed.

Since pumpkins contain so much water, pumpkin filling is quite wet. Everything you bake will therefore be moist. Don't let this worry you. If you follow these recipes carefully, you should have some nice dishes to share with family and friends.

Tips Before You Begin

1. Make sure you have all the ingredients and necessary equipment.

2. "Shortening" means softened margarine, softened butter, or vegetable oil. You can use each in place of the other, unless the recipe calls for one kind only.

3. Flour: all-purpose, presifted flour is best.

4. It's easier to beat eggs with a fork or a whisk than with an eggbeater.

5. To whip cream, beat it with an eggbeater or electric mixer until it's stiff.

6. To sift, place ingredients in a sieve over a bowl. Take a spoon and stir ingredients until they pass through the holes in the sieve to the bowl beneath.

7. When using canned pumpkin filling, read the ingredients on the label. If the manufacturer has added sugar and spices, the results in the following recipes will be sweeter than if you use your own filling.

8. Preheat oven for 20 minutes before cooking.

9. Clean up the kitchen as you work.

Caution

Here are a few basic rules about safety:

1. Ask a grown-up to help you when you:
  a) light the oven or burners.
  b) boil things on top of the stove.
  c) use an electric mixer or blender.
  d) cut a pumpkin into pieces.

2. Set hot pots and pans down on a wooden chopping board, since some counter tops scorch easily.

3. Turn the handles of hot pots and pans away from where people might bump into them.

4. Use potholders when handling anything hot.

Pumpkin Fillings

You can buy pumpkin filling in a store. However, if you want to make your own, there are three ways of doing so.

One small sugar pumpkin ($3\frac{1}{2}$ lbs. or 1.6 kg) makes about 4 cups (.95 l) of cooked pumpkin and $\frac{3}{4}$ cup (180 ml) of seeds.

Equipment:

Paring knife

Metal mixing spoon

Colander or sieve

Small amount of shortening to grease sheet

Cookie sheet, shallow baking pan, or small saucepan

BAKED PUMPKIN PIECES

1. Preheat oven to 325° F (165° C).
2. Use paring knife to cut off top of pumpkin.
3. Use metal spoon to scrape away stringy pulp and seeds.
4. Cut pumpkin into small pieces.

5. Wash pumpkin pieces in cold water. Place them on greased cookie sheet.
6. Bake for an hour, or until soft.
7. Remove from oven and cool.
8. Cut pulp away from skin.
9. Strain pulp through sieve or colander to get rid of lumps.

BAKED WHOLE PUMPKIN

1. Preheat oven to 350° F (177° C).
2. Use paring knife to cut off top of pumpkin, keeping stem in place. Set top aside.
3. Use metal spoon to scrape out stringy pulp and seeds.
4. Replace top and put pumpkin in greased shallow baking pan.
5. Bake for 1½ hours.
6. Remove pumpkin from oven. Pour out water that has collected on bottom.
7. Cool.
8. Cut pulp away from skin and strain through sieve or colander to get rid of lumps.

BOILED PUMPKIN PIECES

1. Use paring knife to cut pumpkin in half.
2. Use metal spoon to scrape away stringy pulp and seeds.
3. Cut shells into 1-inch (2.5 cm) pieces.
4. Cover with boiling water in small saucepan and cook over medium heat from 30 to 45 minutes, until pieces are tender.
5. Cut pulp away from skin and strain through sieve or colander to get rid of lumps.

❧ Roasted Pumpkin Seeds

Ingredients:
1½ tbs. (22 ml) vegetable oil
1 tsp. (5 ml) salt
2 cups (480 ml) pumpkin seeds

Equipment:
Measuring spoons and cup
Mixing spoon
Mixing bowl
Cookie sheet
Colander

What you do:
1. Preheat oven to 250° F (120° C).
2. Wash seeds under warm water in colander.
3. Mix together in bowl: seeds, salt, shortening.
4. Spread seeds on cookie sheet.
5. Bake for 30 minutes, or until golden brown and crispy. Use spoon to stir seeds from time to time while baking.

Chocolate Chip Pumpkin Squares

Ingredients:
2¼ cups (540 ml) flour
2¼ tsp. (11.25 ml) baking powder
½ tsp. (2.5 ml) baking soda
1 tsp. (5 ml) cinnamon
½ tsp. (2.5 ml) nutmeg
4 beaten eggs
1 cup (240 ml) granulated sugar
1 cup (240 ml) brown sugar
½ cup (120 ml) shortening
2 cups (480 ml) pumpkin filling
1 cup (240 ml) chocolate chips

Equipment:
Measuring spoons and cup
Mixing spoon
Fork for beating eggs
Two large mixing bowls
Sieve
Small amount of shortening to grease pan
Rectangular baking pan—9″ × 13″ × 2″ (22.5 × 32.5 × 5 cm)

What you do:
1. Preheat oven to 325° F (165° C).
2. Grease pan.

3. Sift together in one bowl: flour, baking powder, baking soda, cinnamon, nutmeg.

4. Beat eggs in other bowl. Add granulated sugar, brown sugar, shortening, pumpkin filling. Mix.

5. Add flour mixture to sugar mixture. Blend.

6. Add chocolate chips.

7. Pour mixture into pan.

8. Bake for 45 minutes.

9. Allow to cool for 15 minutes. Then cut into squares.

✃§Pumpkin Raisin Cookies

Ingredients:
2½ cups (600 ml) flour
1½ tsp. (7.5 ml) baking soda
½ tsp. (2.5 ml) salt
1½ tsp. (7.5 ml) cinnamon
½ tsp. (2.5 ml) nutmeg
2 beaten eggs
1 cup (240 ml) brown sugar
½ cup (120 ml) granulated sugar
½ cup (120 ml) shortening
1 cup (240 ml) pumpkin filling
1 tsp. (5 ml) vanilla extract
½ cup (120 ml) milk
1 cup (240 ml) chopped walnuts (see below)
1 cup (240 ml) raisins

Equipment:
Measuring spoons and cup
Mixing spoon
Fork for beating eggs
Nut chopper
Cutting board
Sieve
Two large mixing bowls
Small amount of shortening to grease sheet
Cookie sheet

What you do:
1. Preheat oven to 350° F (177° C).
2. Grease cookie sheet.
3. Chop nuts on board.
4. Sift together in large bowl: flour, baking soda, salt, cinnamon, nutmeg.
5. Beat eggs in other bowl. Add brown sugar, granulated sugar, shortening, pumpkin filling, vanilla extract, milk. Mix.
6. Add flour mixture to sugar mixture. Blend.
7. Add nuts and raisins.
8. Drop by spoonfuls onto cookie sheet.
9. Bake 15–18 minutes. Makes 60 cookies.

✑ Pumpkin Ice Cream

Ingredients:
½ pint (240 ml) heavy cream
1 pint (480 ml) vanilla ice cream
1 cup (240 ml) pumpkin filling
½ cup (120 ml) chopped walnuts (see below)
1 tsp. (5 ml) cinnamon
½ tsp. (2.5 ml) nutmeg
½ tsp. (2.5 ml) ginger
½ tsp. (2.5 ml) salt

Equipment:
Measuring spoons and cup
Mixing spoon
Nut chopper
Cutting board
Eggbeater or electric mixer
Small mixing bowl
Large mixing bowl
Four dessert bowls

What you do:
1. Allow ice cream to soften at room temperature for ½ hour before beginning.

2. Use eggbeater or electric mixer to whip cream in small mixing bowl. Store in refrigerator.

3. Chop nuts on board.

4. Place all ingredients except whipped cream in large bowl and mix together.

5. Pour mixture into dessert bowls.

6. Freeze.

7. Serve with whipped cream on top.

~§ Pumpkin Pudding

Ingredients:

4 beaten eggs

1 cup (240 ml) milk

2 cups (480 ml) pumpkin filling

3 tbs. (45 ml) honey

1 tsp. (5 ml) vanilla extract

2 tsp. (10 ml) cinnamon

½ tsp. (2.5 ml) ginger

1 tsp. (5 ml) nutmeg

½ tsp. (2.5 ml) salt

½ cup (120 ml) raisins

Equipment:
Measuring spoons and cup
Knife
Mixing spoon
Fork for beating eggs
Small mixing bowl
Large mixing bowl
Small amount of shortening to grease dish
1 qt. (.95 l) casserole dish

What you do:
1. Preheat oven to 350° F (177° C).
2. Grease casserole dish.
3. Beat eggs in small mixing bowl.
4. Pour all ingredients into large bowl and mix thoroughly.
5. Pour into casserole dish.
6. Bake for about an hour, or until a knife blade comes out clean when poked into middle.

✑ Pumpkin Pie

CRUST

Ingredients:
½ cup (120 ml) softened margarine
1 3-oz. (85 g) package softened cream cheese
1 cup (240 ml) flour

Equipment:
Measuring cup
Mixing spoon
Mixing bowl
Small amount of shortening to grease pan
9-in. (22.5 cm) pie pan

What you do:
1. Grease pan.
2. Mix ingredients together.
3. Press into pie pan, using fingertips.

FILLING
Ingredients:
1 cup (240 ml) brown sugar
½ tsp. (2.5 ml) salt
½ tsp. (2.5 ml) cinnamon
¼ tsp. (1.25 ml) nutmeg
2 beaten eggs
1½ cups (360 ml) pumpkin filling
1½ cups (360 ml) evaporated milk
½ cup (120 ml) heavy cream

Equipment:
Measuring spoons and cup
Knife
Mixing spoon
Fork for beating eggs
Eggbeater
Small mixing bowl
Two large mixing bowls

What you do:

1. Preheat oven to 350° F (177° C).

2. Beat eggs in small mixing bowl.

3. Place all ingredients except cream in large bowl and mix together.

4. Pour into pie crust.

5. Bake for 40 minutes, or until firm. It's done if a knife blade comes out clean when poked into middle.

6. Use eggbeater to whip cream in other large bowl.

7. After pie has cooled, serve with whipped cream on top.

ঙ§Pumpkin Layer Cake

Ingredients:

4 beaten eggs
4⅓ cups (1 1 + 40 ml) flour
2 cups (480 ml) sugar
2 tsp. (10 ml) baking soda
3 tsp. (15 ml) baking powder
1 tsp. (5 ml) salt
3 tsp. (15 ml) cinnamon
½ tsp. (2.5 ml) nutmeg
1 cup (240 ml) shortening
2 cups (480 ml) pumpkin filling
1 cup (240 ml) chopped pecans or walnuts (see below)

Equipment:

Measuring spoons and cup

Knife

Mixing spoon

Fork for beating eggs

Nut chopper

Cutting board

Sieve

Two large mixing bowls

Small amount of shortening to grease cake pans

Two 9-inch (22.5 cm) single layer cake pans

Two wire racks

What you do:

1. Preheat oven to 350° F (177° C).
2. Grease pans.
3. Chop nuts on board.
4. Sift together in large bowl: flour, sugar, baking soda, baking powder, salt, cinnamon, and nutmeg.
5. Beat eggs in other bowl. Add shortening and pumpkin filling. Mix.
6. Add flour mixture to egg mixture. Blend.
7. Add nuts.
8. Divide mixture between cake pans.
9. Bake for 30–40 minutes. It's done if a knife blade comes out clean when poked into middle.
10. Let cool in pans for 10 minutes.

11. Remove cakes from pans by turning pans upside down on wire racks. Let cake cool completely—about ½ hour.

FROSTING

Ingredients:
2 egg whites (see below)
⅓ cup (80 ml) softened butter
1 tsp. (5 ml) vanilla extract
¼ tsp. (1.25 ml) salt
2 tbs. (30 ml) grated orange peel (from real orange—see below)
4 cups (.95 l) sifted confectioners sugar
¼ cup (60 ml) milk
Orange food coloring
1 cup (240 ml) semisweet chocolate bits

Equipment:
Measuring spoons and cup
Mixing spoon
Fork
Small mixing bowls
Two large mixing bowls
Sieve
Grater
Wax paper to put under grater
Spatula

What you do:

1. Separate egg whites from yolks. Do this by breaking each egg over small mixing bowl. Gently slide yolk back and forth between two shell halves, letting white dribble into bowl beneath. Freeze egg yolks for later use.

2. Grate 2 tbs. (30 ml) of orange peel by moving orange back and forth against side of grater.

3. Sift 4 cups (.95 l) of confectioners' sugar into large mixing bowl.

4. Mash butter against sides of other large mixing bowl with back of mixing spoon.

5. Add vanilla, salt, orange peel, and 1 cup (240 ml) sugar to butter.

6. While stirring with fork, add some of egg whites, some more of sugar, then more of egg whites, more of sugar, and so on, until sugar and egg whites are used up.

7. If mixture is too thick to spread, add a little milk.

8. Add a few drops of orange food coloring.

9. Using spatula, frost the top of the first layer. Then carefully put second layer on top and frost it. Frost sides.

10. Use chocolate bits to make face.

⊷ꜱPumpkin Bread

Ingredients:
1½ cups (360 ml) flour
1 tsp. (5 ml) baking soda
1½ tsp. (7.5 ml) salt
1 tsp. (5 ml) nutmeg
2 tsp. (10 ml) cinnamon
½ tsp. (2.5 ml) ginger
2 beaten eggs
½ cup (120 ml) chopped pecans (see below)
1 cup (240 ml) pumpkin filling
½ cup (120 ml) shortening

Equipment:
Measuring spoons and cup
Knife
Mixing spoon
Fork for beating eggs
Nut chopper
Cutting board
Sieve
Two large mixing bowls
Small amount of shortening to grease pan
Loaf pan—9″ × 5″ × 3″ (22.5 × 12.5 × 7.5 cm)
Wire rack

What you do:

1. Preheat oven to 350° F (177° C).

2. Grease pan.

3. Chop nuts on board.

4. Sift together in large mixing bowl: flour, baking soda, salt, nutmeg, cinnamon, ginger.

5. Add pecans.

6. Beat eggs in other bowl. Add pumpkin filling and shortening.

7. Add flour mixture to egg mixture. Blend.

8. Pour mixture into pan.

9. Bake for 1 hour. It's done if a knife blade comes out clean when poked into middle.

10. Let it cool in pan for 10 minutes.

11. Turn pan upside down on wire rack. Let bread cool for about ½ hour. It's best if eaten 24 hours later.

∼§ Pumpkin Soup

Ingredients:
2 beaten egg yolks (see below)
2 cups (480 ml) pumpkin filling
1 10-oz. (300 ml) can beef consommé soup, undiluted
½ cup (120 ml) heavy cream
Salt and pepper
1 tsp. (5 ml) onion powder
Dash of nutmeg
Chopped parsley, dried or fresh

Equipment:
Measuring spoons and cup
Mixing spoon
Fork for beating yolks
Two small mixing bowls
Saucepan

What you do:
1. Separate egg whites from yolks. Do this by breaking each egg over small mixing bowl. Gently slide yolk back and forth between two shell halves, letting white dribble into bowl beneath. Drop the yolks into other mixing bowl and beat them with fork. Freeze egg whites for later use.
2. Add cream to egg yolks, blend and set aside.
3. In saucepan, mix pumpkin filling and consommé.

4. Light burner, and heat ingredients in saucepan over medium heat until they boil.

5. Add cream and egg mixture and stir briskly until soup thickens. Don't let it boil.

6. Season with salt, pepper, onion powder, and a dash of nutmeg.

7. Sprinkle with parsley and serve. If this soup is too thick, thin it with a little milk. Some people like their soup served in a hollowed-out pumpkin shell.

ᵛᵍPumpkin Pancakes

Ingredients:
2 cups (480 ml) flour
1 tsp. (5 ml) baking soda
½ tsp. (2.5 ml) salt
1 tsp. (5 ml) cinnamon
¼ tsp. (1.25 ml) ginger
¼ tsp. (1.25 ml) nutmeg
2 tsp. (10 ml) baking powder
2 beaten eggs
¼ cup (60 ml) shortening
¼ cup (60 ml) water
1½ cups (360 ml) buttermilk
1 cup (240 ml) pumpkin filling
Maple syrup

Equipment:
Measuring spoons and cup
Mixing spoon
Fork for beating eggs
Sieve
Two large mixing bowls
Enough shortening to coat bottom of pan lightly
Large frying pan
Spatula

What you do:
1. Sift together in large mixing bowl: flour, baking soda, salt, cinnamon, ginger, nutmeg, baking powder.
2. Beat eggs with fork in other bowl. Add shortening, water, buttermilk, and pumpkin filling. Mix.
3. Add flour mixture to egg mixture. Blend.
4. Turn burner onto medium-high under frying pan. Add enough shortening just to coat bottom of pan. Pan is hot enough if drops of water "dance" when you sprinkle them on bottom.
5. Drop spoonfuls of batter into pan.
6. Fry pancakes on first side until small bubbles appear. Then turn with spatula to fry on other side.
7. Remove and serve immediately with maple syrup.

Pumpkin Hamburgers

Ingredients:
2 tbs. (30 ml) ketchup
2 slices of bread, cubed
1 small onion, sliced
1 lb. (454 g) ground beef
¼ cup (120 ml) pumpkin filling
Dash of salt, pepper, nutmeg
Hamburger buns

Equipment:
Paring knife
Measuring spoons and cup
Mixing spoon
Large mixing bowl
Enough shortening to grease pan
Frying pan

What you do:
1. Grease pan.
2. Cut the bread into cubes.
3. Use paring knife to slice onion.
4. Mix ingredients in large bowl.
5. Shape into four patties.
6. Heat frying pan on burner.
7. Fry patties on both sides.
8. Serve on buns.

❧ Pumpkin Squash

Ingredients:
1 whole pumpkin
Brown sugar
Butter

Equipment:
Paring knife
Metal spoon
Cookie sheet

What you do:
1. Preheat oven to 350° F (177° C).
2. Cut pumpkin in half.
3. Scrape out pulp and seeds, so that the sides are smooth.
4. Cut halves in half, so that you have four quarters.
5. Pour just enough water onto cookie sheet to cover bottom.
6. Place pumpkin quarters on cookie sheet, skin side down.
7. Coat tops with brown sugar and globs of butter.
8. Bake 1½ hours.

❧Pumpkin Health Shake

Ingredients:
1 lb. (454 g) plain yogurt
¾ cup (180 ml) pumpkin filling
1½ tbs. (15ml) honey
1½ tsp. (7.5 ml) nutmeg
1½ cups (360 ml) milk
2 tbs. (30 ml) wheat germ

Equipment:
Measuring spoons and cup
Mixing spoon
Large mixing bowl
Blender, if possible
Three tall glasses
Plastic wrap

What you do:
1. Combine ingredients in blender, or mix in bowl.
2. Pour into glasses.
3. Cover with plastic wrap and chill.

Party Ideas and Crafts Projects

Before You Begin

The following activities can be done in groups. Sometimes, it's fun to give a crafts party for family and friends. While one person mixes powder paint with water, another person can be cutting shapes out of paper. Hammering, measuring, carving more pumpkins—these things take a lot of work. It's a good idea to ask an adult to help. You'll need plenty of newspaper to put underneath the materials you're using. Also, it's good to wear an apron. Crafts projects are sometimes messy and can take up a lot of space. And don't forget to clean up when you're finished!

◄§Jack-o'-lantern Invitation

Equipment:
Black construction paper, 9" wide × 12" long (22.5 × 30 cm)
Corrugated paper from light-bulb cartons
Scissors
Glue
Orange poster or powder paint
Paintbrush
Black and orange felt-tip markers or crayons

What you do:
1. Draw a pumpkin, 3" × 3" (7.5 × 7.5 cm), on smooth side of corrugated paper.
2. Cut it out.

3. Paint corrugated side orange. Set it aside to dry.
4. Fold construction paper lengthwise in two, so each section is 4½" wide × 12" long (11.25 × 30 cm). Cut along folded line. Now fold each of these sections in half, so you have two blank invitations, 6" wide × 4½" long (15 × 11.25 cm).
5. Draw features with black marker on flat, unpainted side of corrugated pumpkin.

6. Cut them out.

7. Glue smooth side of "jack-o'-lantern" to front of card.

8. Using orange marker or crayon, write COME TO A PARTY across top.

9. On inside, write place and time.

❧Pumpkin Place Card

Equipment:
Orange construction paper, 9″ × 12″ (22.5 × 30 cm)
Scissors
Glue
Black felt-tip marker
Three pipe cleaners
Spool

What you do:
1. Cut two small pumpkins and a rectangle out of construction paper.

2. Write the guest's name on the rectangle.

3. Draw features on the pumpkins.

4. Glue pumpkins and rectangle to pipe cleaners.

5. Color the spool black with felt-tip marker.

6. Stick the pipe cleaners into the spool.

❧ Pumpkin Person

Equipment:
Old shirt and pair of pants
Scarf
Wads of newspaper or leaves
Safety pins
Pumpkin
Pencil
Black felt-tip marker
2 three-foot (90 cm) stakes
Hammer
Nails
Flat piece of wood (big enough to support a pumpkin)
Box

What you do:
1. Pin closed the ends of shirt sleeves and pants legs.
2. Button the shirt.
3. Stuff the pants and shirt separately with wads of newspaper or leaves.
4. Pin shirt to pants at several points around waist.
5. Add more stuffing, if necessary, to make a solid body.
6. Make head out of pumpkin. Create a face with a pencil and trace the outline with marker.

78

7. Stick stakes into ground next to each other.

8. Place wood on top of stakes. Nail it down.

9. Put box in front of stakes and seat body on it.

10. Adjust height of stakes so platform is just above pumpkin person's shoulders.

11. Nail back of shirt collar to edge of platform.

12. Place pumpkin head on platform over shoulders.

13. Hide platform's edge with scarf and nail it down so it won't blow away.

·§Pumpkin Totem Pole

Equipment:
Three pumpkins—small, medium, large

Felt-tip markers or pencil

Large mixing bowl

Metal mixing spoon

Small (paring) knife

Big knife

Bowl

Broomstick handle, or any long stick

Three flashlights

What you do:
1. Line up 3 pumpkins, with smallest one first.
2. Carve a face in each one.
3. Remove lids.
4. Cut holes the size of the stick in bottoms of pumpkins 1 and 2.
5. Pile pumpkins on top of each other: 3 goes on bottom, 2 in middle, and 1 on top.

6. Light up faces by putting flashlight inside each pumpkin.

7. Stick broomstick handle or stick through holes in pumpkins 1 and 2 and into bottom of pumpkin 3.

8. Windowsills and porches make good places for totem poles.

✌ Pumpkin-Seed Mask

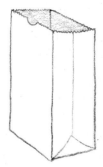

Equipment:
Paper bag that will fit over your head
Pumpkin seeds
Scissors
Pencil
Glue
Powder or poster paint
Paintbrush

What you do:

1. Paint bag and let it dry.

2. Draw a face on one side. Glue down pumpkin seeds on features.

3. Cut out eyes.

4. For a more elaborate mask, paint some small boxes. Glue them onto the bag as noses, ears, and eyes.

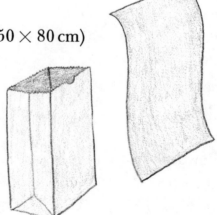

✑Pumpkin Costume

Equipment:
Orange crepe paper, 20″ × 32″ (50 × 80 cm)
Brown grocery bag
Scissors
Black felt-tip marker
Safety pin
Orange powder or poster paint
Paintbrush

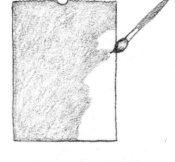

What you do:

1. Put bag over head. The bottom should come to top of shoulders. If it's too long, cut to fit.

2. Paint bag orange.

3. When paint dries, draw features on bag with marker. Make sure eyes line up with your own.

4. Cut out eyes.

5. Use crepe paper as cape. Fasten it in front with safety pin.

~§ Dancing Pumpkin Person

Equipment:
Orange and black construction paper, 9″ × 12″ (22.5 × 30 cm)
Scissors
Glue
Crayons or felt-tip markers
Black thread, 12″ (30 cm) long

What you do:
1. Draw a pumpkin on orange construction paper.
2. Cut it out.
3. Draw features and stem on black construction paper. Cut them out and paste them to pumpkin.

4. Make legs by cutting out two strips, 1″ wide × 12″ long (2.5 × 30 cm), from black construction paper. Fold them up like an accordion. Glue one end of each strip to bottom of pumpkin for legs.

84

5. Make arms the same way, only use strips that are 1″ wide × 9″ long (2.5 × 22.5 cm). Paste one end of each strip to either side of face.

6. Draw hands and feet on orange construction paper. Cut them out and glue them to ends of arms and legs.

7. Add hair with felt-tip marker.

8. Poke a tiny hole through stem and stick one end of thread through. Tie two ends of thread together.

9. Hang pumpkin person from hook on wall.

✑Strip Lantern

Equipment:

8 strips of orange construction paper, 1″ wide × 18″ long (2.5 × 45 cm)

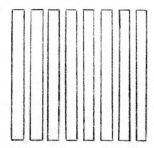

Colored construction paper (including green), 9″ wide × 12″ long (22.5 × 30 cm)

Scissors

Pencil

Two one-inch (2.5 cm) roundheaded paper fasteners

Glue

Stapler

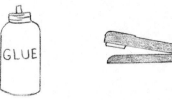

What you do:

1. Place 8 strips on top of each other. Punch a hole through the center of all of them.

2. Run paper fastener through center hole of strips from top. Secure fastener loosely.

86

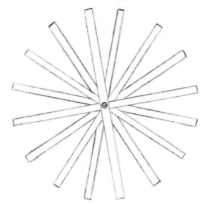

3. Spread strips in circle, with even spaces between. Tighten fastener so strips hardly move.

4. Take ends of strips and pull them up together so they meet at top.

5. Stick other paper fastener through ends, and secure it so ends are held firmly in place.

6. Cut a strip of green construction paper, ¾″ wide × 12″ long (1.9 × 30 cm). Staple ends together to make handle for lantern.

7. Draw two leaves on green construction paper. Cut them out and staple or glue to handle.

8. Staple or glue handle to top of lantern.

9. Draw eyes, nose, and mouth on colored construction paper. Cut them out and glue or staple them to front of lantern.

Pumpkin Toy

Equipment:
Black and orange construction paper, 9″ wide × 12″ long (22.5 × 30 cm)
Scissors
Glue
Crayons or felt-tip markers
Pencil
One-inch (2.5 cm) roundheaded paper fasteners
Stapler

What you do:
1. Draw a pumpkin head, 2″ round (5 cm), with a long neck, 1″ wide × 3½″ long (2.5 × 8.8 cm), on orange construction paper. Draw in features. Cut out head and neck.

2. Also on orange paper, draw a pumpkin shape for the body, 6″ round (15 cm). Cut it out.

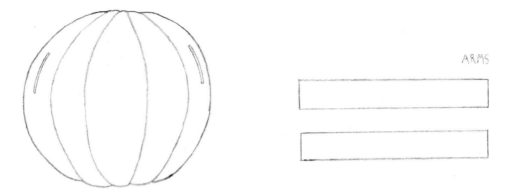

3. Make two 1¼″ slits (3.12 cm) on either side of pumpkin body so paper arms can be slipped through later on.

4. Draw two arms on orange paper, 1″ wide × 6″ long (2.5 × 15 cm), and cut them out.

5. Stick ends through slits in body. Make sure ends overlap at the middle of the body.

6. Place body on head and neck, with end of neck in back of overlapping arm ends. Push paper fastener through, overlapping arm ends and end of neck, and secure it in place.

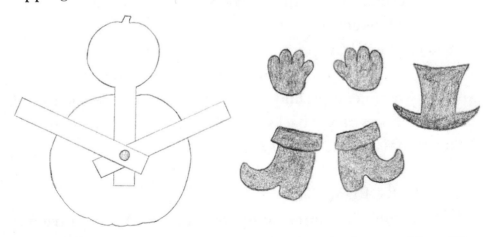

7. On black construction paper, draw hands, feet, and hat. Cut them out and glue them in place on the arms and body.

8. As you move the head from side to side, arms will go up and down.

GAMES

There are lots of games you can make up using pumpkins. Here are a few ideas to get you started. See if you can make up some more.

PUMPKIN HUNT

Hide several pumpkins in good spots. Whoever finds the most pumpkins gets a prize.

You can also draw pumpkins on construction paper and cut them out. Write a number on the back of each one. Hide them, and ask your friends to find them. Then ask each person to add up the numbers on the backs of the pumpkins they've gathered. Whoever has the most points wins.

LEAPFROG PUMPKIN

Place a number of large pumpkins in a row. Ask your friends to jump over them without touching their surface. Whoever touches has to drop out.

Pumpkin Jokes

What does a pumpkin sew?
A pumpkin patch.

What do pumpkins eat at ball games?
Pulp corn.

What vegetable does a pumpkin turn into when an elephant steps on it?
Squash.

What do pumpkins eat at McDonald's?
Big Max.

What did the pumpkin say after Thanksgiving?
Good pie.

What did the orange pumpkin say to the green pumpkin?
Why orange you orange?

What do pumpkin poets write?
Rinds.

What did the pumpkin say to his girl friend?
"I seed you with another guy."

What did a mad pumpkin say to his enemy?
"I'll stem on your foot!"

What's orange and goes *bzzzzzzz?*
An electric pumpkin.

When asked how he was, what did the pumpkin reply?
"I'm vine, thank you."

What did one jack-o'-lantern say to another?
"Cut it out!"

What kind of romances do pumpkins have?
Mushy.

What's orange and flies?
Super Pumpkin.

What was orange and lived in Egypt?
Tutapumpkin.

What does a pumpkin pie say after a big meal?
"That was filling."

What's a pumpkin's favorite sport?
Squash.

What does a pumpkin tiger do?
   Stalk its prey.

What does a pumpkin priest stand on?
   A pulpit.

What's orange and goes *putt-putt-putt?*
   An outboard pumpkin.

A. "What's the difference between a pumpkin and a mailbox?"
B. "I don't know."
A. "If you don't know, I'm never going to ask you to mail a letter!"

Index

About the Author

MARGERY CUYLER received her B.A. from Sarah Lawrence College, where she specialized in children's literature. She became a pumpkin enthusiast at the age of eight, when she carved her first jack-o'-lantern with the help of her older brothers and sister. Every year since then, she has celebrated Halloween with a great pumpkin-carving and cooking party.

The children's book editor at a publishing house, Ms. Cuyler lives in New York City. She is also the author of *Jewish Holidays*.

About the Illustrator

CORBETT JONES is a free-lance illustrator who lives in New York City.